Military Research Records:

A Family Tree Research Workbook

Written By Catherine Coulter

Military Research Records: A Family Tree Research Workbook

Copyright © 2013 Catherine Coulter

All rights reserved

ISBN-13: 978-1484833759

ISBN-10: 1484833759

Books Written By Catherine Coulter

My Family Tree Research Records

Family Group Research Records

Census Research Records

Cemetery and Funeral Home Research Records

Court House Research Records

Web Log and Web Accounts

Naturalization Research Records

Military Research Records

My Family Tree Notebook

Immigration Research Records

Internet Addresses and Accounts

Books Written by Catherine Coulter under the name of Cathy Coulter

The Man in Red

A Children's Book of Poems Goodnight and Hello

Information on an ancestor's military record can be very helpful in gathering facts on not only that particular ancestor but also about his family as well. If you can gather enough facts on his military service you may be able to obtain his service record from the United States National Archives. You may also learn enough to trace his movements throughout the war, any wounds, or mishaps he may have encountered on the way. If he was involved in any of the wars major battles you may even be able to trace his movements during them as well. The major battle fields in America like Gettysburg may very well have information on your ancestor, monuments to his regiment, and company with his name listed.

The United States National Archives has service records from the Revolutionary War till World War 1 that you may be able to order for a fee. Now from World War 1 forward, you either need to be the service man or woman or the next of kin to obtain information on them. Though, going backwards you should be able to order the records. You will need to fill out a form either on line or through the mail to request the information and pay a fee. The more information that you have on your ancestor the more likely the National Archives will be able to find the records you are looking for. The service records can sometimes be quite detailed from what dates they enrolled or were drafted and date of discharge to the wounds they received, battles they were in, and more. You may be able to get pension records for them as well. Pension records will give you information on them and their families after the war such as residence, occupation, members of the family, dates and possibly their health.

When researching for military information the first place to head would be to talk to relatives to see if they know any information about the military service in the family. Then using the internet search engines can be of help by putting in the ancestor's name and some of the information you have gathered. For example, when I put James L. Griffin Civil War Pennsylvania into a search engine, this is one of several sites that was the result: 140th Pennsylvania Infantry Soldier Roster - Civil War Index www.civilwarindex.com/armypa/.../140th_pa_infantry_roster.pdf. The more or different combinations of information you put into the search engine you may be lucky enough to get a lot of results.

There are many internet sites devoted to the wars. Some of the regiments and companies from the wars have their own sites. Historical societies, libraries, and state and county history books sometimes will have military rosters you can look through and information on the various wars. The newspapers are another source of military information. They often, during war time, mentioned units/companies and the men attached to them so don't forget to check them out.

There is a place in the back of this book for you to add web sites you are using. Below is log for your ancestors name and the war he was involved in. That will help you to find the worksheet you used for him. Military Research Records will help you gather the information on your ancestor's military service and pension records. You will find in this book spaces for you to add the rank, company, regiment/vessel, enlistment date, discharge date, and more. There is also a place for pension information.

	Last Name	First Name	War
1			
2			
3			
4			
5			
6			
7			
8			
9			
10			
11			
12			
13			
14			
15			
16			
17			
18			
19			
20			
21			
22			
23			
24			
25			
26			
27			
28			

Ancestor's Name	
Birth Date	Death Date
Enlistment Age	Residence
Occupation	Employer

Drafted	Enlisted	Registration
Date of Enlistment	Date of Discharge	
Rank	Company	
Regiment/Vessel		
Unit		
Commanding Officer		

Service/ Battles

Honors and Awards

War Medals

Pension	Date	Next of Kin
State		
County		
Residence at time of Pension		

Ancestor's Name	
Birth Date	Death Date
Enlistment Age	Residence
Occupation	Employer

Drafted	Enlisted	Registration
Date of Enlistment	Date of Discharge	
Rank	Company	
Regiment/Vessel		
Unit		
Commanding Officer		

Service/ Battles

Honors and Awards

War Medals

Pension	Date	Next of Kin
State		
County		
Residence at time of Pension		

Ancestor's Name	
Birth Date	Death Date
Enlistment Age	Residence
Occupation	Employer

Drafted	Enlisted	Registration
Date of Enlistment	Date of Discharge	
Rank	Company	
Regiment/Vessel		
Unit		
Commanding Officer		

Service/ Battles

Honors and Awards

War Medals

Pension	Date	Next of Kin
State		
County		
Residence at time of Pension		

Ancestor's Name	
Birth Date	Death Date
Enlistment Age	Residence
Occupation	Employer

Drafted	Enlisted	Registration
Date of Enlistment	Date of Discharge	
Rank	Company	
Regiment/Vessel		
Unit		
Commanding Officer		

Service/ Battles

Honors and Awards

War Medals

Pension	Date	Next of Kin
State		
County		
Residence at time of Pension		

Ancestor's Name	
Birth Date	Death Date
Enlistment Age	Residence
Occupation	Employer

Drafted	Enlisted	Registration
Date of Enlistment	Date of Discharge	
Rank	Company	
Regiment/Vessel		
Unit		
Commanding Officer		

Service/ Battles

Honors and Awards

War Medals

Pension	Date	Next of Kin
State		
County		
Residence at time of Pension		

Ancestor's Name	
Birth Date	Death Date
Enlistment Age	Residence
Occupation	Employer

Drafted	Enlisted	Registration
Date of Enlistment	Date of Discharge	
Rank	Company	
Regiment/Vessel		
Unit		
Commanding Officer		

Service/ Battles

Honors and Awards

War Medals

Pension	Date	Next of Kin
State		
County		
Residence at time of Pension		

Ancestor's Name	
Birth Date	Death Date
Enlistment Age	Residence
Occupation	Employer

Drafted	Enlisted	Registration
Date of Enlistment		Date of Discharge
Rank		Company
Regiment/Vessel		
Unit		
Commanding Officer		

Service/ Battles

Honors and Awards

War Medals

Pension	Date	Next of Kin
State		
County		
Residence at time of Pension		

Ancestor's Name	
Birth Date	Death Date
Enlistment Age	Residence
Occupation	Employer

Drafted	Enlisted	Registration
Date of Enlistment	Date of Discharge	
Rank	Company	
Regiment/Vessel		
Unit		
Commanding Officer		

Service/ Battles

Honors and Awards

War Medals

Pension	Date	Next of Kin
State		
County		
Residence at time of Pension		

Ancestor's Name	
Birth Date	Death Date
Enlistment Age	Residence
Occupation	Employer

Drafted	Enlisted	Registration
Date of Enlistment	Date of Discharge	
Rank	Company	
Regiment/Vessel		
Unit		
Commanding Officer		

Service/ Battles

Honors and Awards

War Medals

Pension	Date	Next of Kin
State		
County		
Residence at time of Pension		

Ancestor's Name	
Birth Date	Death Date
Enlistment Age	Residence
Occupation	Employer

Drafted	Enlisted	Registration
Date of Enlistment	Date of Discharge	
Rank	Company	
Regiment/Vessel		
Unit		
Commanding Officer		

Service/ Battles

Honors and Awards

War Medals

Pension	Date	Next of Kin
State		
County		
Residence at time of Pension		

Ancestor's Name	
Birth Date	Death Date
Enlistment Age	Residence
Occupation	Employer

Drafted	Enlisted	Registration
Date of Enlistment	Date of Discharge	
Rank	Company	
Regiment/Vessel		
Unit		
Commanding Officer		

Service/ Battles

Honors and Awards

War Medals

Pension	Date	Next of Kin
State		
County		
Residence at time of Pension		

Ancestor's Name	
Birth Date	Death Date
Enlistment Age	Residence
Occupation	Employer

Drafted	Enlisted	Registration
Date of Enlistment		Date of Discharge
Rank		Company
Regiment/Vessel		
Unit		
Commanding Officer		

Service/ Battles

Honors and Awards

War Medals

Pension	Date	Next of Kin
State		
County		
Residence at time of Pension		

Ancestor's Name	
Birth Date	Death Date
Enlistment Age	Residence
Occupation	Employer

Drafted	Enlisted	Registration
Date of Enlistment	Date of Discharge	
Rank	Company	
Regiment/Vessel		
Unit		
Commanding Officer		

Service/ Battles

Honors and Awards

War Medals

Pension	Date	Next of Kin
State		
County		
Residence at time of Pension		

Ancestor's Name	
Birth Date	Death Date
Enlistment Age	Residence
Occupation	Employer

Drafted	Enlisted	Registration
Date of Enlistment	Date of Discharge	
Rank	Company	
Regiment/Vessel		
Unit		
Commanding Officer		

Service/ Battles

Honors and Awards

War Medals

Pension	Date	Next of Kin
State		
County		
Residence at time of Pension		

Ancestor's Name	
Birth Date	Death Date
Enlistment Age	Residence
Occupation	Employer

Drafted	Enlisted	Registration
Date of Enlistment		Date of Discharge
Rank		Company
Regiment/Vessel		
Unit		
Commanding Officer		

Service/ Battles

Honors and Awards

War Medals

Pension	Date	Next of Kin
State		
County		
Residence at time of Pension		

Ancestor's Name	
Birth Date	Death Date
Enlistment Age	Residence
Occupation	Employer

Drafted	Enlisted	Registration
Date of Enlistment	Date of Discharge	
Rank	Company	
Regiment/Vessel		
Unit		
Commanding Officer		

Service/ Battles

Honors and Awards

War Medals

Pension	Date	Next of Kin
State		
County		
Residence at time of Pension		

Ancestor's Name	
Birth Date	Death Date
Enlistment Age	Residence
Occupation	Employer

Drafted	Enlisted	Registration
Date of Enlistment	Date of Discharge	
Rank	Company	
Regiment/Vessel		
Unit		
Commanding Officer		

Service/ Battles

Honors and Awards

War Medals

Pension	Date	Next of Kin
State		
County		
Residence at time of Pension		

Ancestor's Name	
Birth Date	Death Date
Enlistment Age	Residence
Occupation	Employer

Drafted	Enlisted	Registration
Date of Enlistment	Date of Discharge	
Rank	Company	
Regiment/Vessel		
Unit		
Commanding Officer		

Service/ Battles

Honors and Awards

War Medals

Pension	Date	Next of Kin
State		
County		
Residence at time of Pension		

Ancestor's Name	
Birth Date	Death Date
Enlistment Age	Residence
Occupation	Employer

Drafted	Enlisted	Registration
Date of Enlistment	Date of Discharge	
Rank	Company	
Regiment/Vessel		
Unit		
Commanding Officer		

Service/ Battles

Honors and Awards

War Medals

Pension	Date	Next of Kin
State		
County		
Residence at time of Pension		

Ancestor's Name	
Birth Date	Death Date
Enlistment Age	Residence
Occupation	Employer

Drafted	Enlisted	Registration
Date of Enlistment	Date of Discharge	
Rank	Company	
Regiment/Vessel		
Unit		
Commanding Officer		

Service/ Battles

Honors and Awards

War Medals

Pension	Date	Next of Kin
State		
County		
Residence at time of Pension		

Ancestor's Name	
Birth Date	Death Date
Enlistment Age	Residence
Occupation	Employer

Drafted	Enlisted	Registration
Date of Enlistment	Date of Discharge	
Rank	Company	
Regiment/Vessel		
Unit		
Commanding Officer		

Service/ Battles

Honors and Awards

War Medals

Pension	Date	Next of Kin
State		
County		
Residence at time of Pension		

Ancestor's Name	
Birth Date	Death Date
Enlistment Age	Residence
Occupation	Employer

Drafted	Enlisted	Registration
Date of Enlistment	Date of Discharge	
Rank	Company	
Regiment/Vessel		
Unit		
Commanding Officer		

Service/ Battles

Honors and Awards

War Medals

Pension	Date	Next of Kin
State		
County		
Residence at time of Pension		

Ancestor's Name	
Birth Date	Death Date
Enlistment Age	Residence
Occupation	Employer

Drafted	Enlisted	Registration
Date of Enlistment	Date of Discharge	
Rank	Company	
Regiment/Vessel		
Unit		
Commanding Officer		

Service/ Battles

Honors and Awards

War Medals

Pension	Date	Next of Kin
State		
County		
Residence at time of Pension		

Ancestor's Name	
Birth Date	Death Date
Enlistment Age	Residence
Occupation	Employer

Drafted	Enlisted	Registration
Date of Enlistment		Date of Discharge
Rank		Company
Regiment/Vessel		
Unit		
Commanding Officer		

Service/ Battles

Honors and Awards

War Medals

Pension	Date	Next of Kin
State		
County		
Residence at time of Pension		

Ancestor's Name	
Birth Date	Death Date
Enlistment Age	Residence
Occupation	Employer

Drafted	Enlisted	Registration
Date of Enlistment	Date of Discharge	
Rank	Company	
Regiment/Vessel		
Unit		
Commanding Officer		

Service/ Battles

Honors and Awards

War Medals

Pension	Date	Next of Kin
State		
County		
Residence at time of Pension		

Ancestor's Name	
Birth Date	Death Date
Enlistment Age	Residence
Occupation	Employer

Drafted	Enlisted	Registration
Date of Enlistment	Date of Discharge	
Rank	Company	
Regiment/Vessel		
Unit		
Commanding Officer		

Service/ Battles

Honors and Awards

War Medals

Pension	Date	Next of Kin
State		
County		
Residence at time of Pension		

Ancestor's Name	
Birth Date	Death Date
Enlistment Age	Residence
Occupation	Employer

Drafted	Enlisted	Registration
Date of Enlistment	Date of Discharge	
Rank	Company	
Regiment/Vessel		
Unit		
Commanding Officer		

Service/ Battles

Honors and Awards

War Medals

Pension	Date	Next of Kin
State		
County		
Residence at time of Pension		

Web Sites Used